Axolotls for Kids: Beyond the Gills

Discover The World of Axolotls With Fascinating Facts, Amazing Photos, and Everything You Need to Know!

CHARLOTTE GIBBS

© Copyright 2024 - All rights reserved.

The content contained within this book may not be reproduced, duplicated, or transmitted without direct written permission from the author or the publisher.

Under no circumstances will any blame or legal responsibility be held against the publisher or author for any damages, reparation, or monetary loss due to the information contained within this book, either directly or indirectly.

Legal Notice:
This book is copyright-protected. It is only for personal use. You cannot amend, distribute, sell, use, quote, or paraphrase any part of the content within this book without the consent of the author or publisher.

Disclaimer Notice:
Please note the information contained within this document is for educational and entertainment purposes only. Every effort has been executed to present accurate, up-to-date, reliable, and complete information. No warranties of any kind are declared or implied. Readers acknowledge that the author is not engaged in rendering legal, financial, medical, or professional advice. The content within this book has been derived from various sources. Please consult a licensed professional before attempting any techniques outlined in this book.

By reading this document, the reader agrees that under no circumstances is the author responsible for any losses, direct or indirect, that are incurred as a result of the use of the information contained within this document, including, but not limited to, errors, omissions, or inaccuracies.

Table of Contents

Introduction — Axolotls are Awesome!   5

CHAPTER 1

Axolotls & Their Amazing Amphibian Friends!   7

Axolotls: The Mexican Marvel   8

Other Amazing Amphibians   10

Tiger Salamander: Axolotl's Cousins   11

Frogs and Toads: Leaping Relatives   11

CHAPTER 2

Axolotl Anatomy: Discover Their Wiggly Parts   15

Gills: Breathing Underwater   16

Limbs: Tiny Feet, Big Moves   17

Skin: Smooth & Slimy   19

CHAPTER 3

Axolotl Habitat: Their Magical Water Worlds   23

Lakes and Canals: Home Sweet Home   24

Aquariums: Welcome Axolotls to Their New Splashy Home!   25

CHAPTER 4

Yummy Eats for Axolotls: What's on Their Menu?   29

Insects and Worms: Yummy Protein   30

Fishy Delights: A Special Treat for Aquatic Friends   31

Cannibalism: It's Getting Too Crowded in Here! 31
Pellet Power: Tasty Bites 32

CHAPTER 5
Axolotl Antics: Discover Their Funny Behaviors 35
Regeneration: Best Skill Ever 36
Sneaky Predators: The Ultimate Hide-and-Gulp Hunters! 37
Social Life: Solitary but Curious 38

CHAPTER 6
Axolotl Life Cycle: From Tiny Egg to Underwater Superstar 41
Eggs: The Beginning of Life 42
Larvae: Growing Up Underwater 43
Adulthood: Axolotls Stay Young Forever! 43

CHAPTER 7
Axolotl Superheroes: Battling the Threats They Face 47
Habitat Destruction: Axolotls Going Homeless? 48
Pollution: A Silent Killer 49
Exotic Fish: Unwelcome Competition 49
Sneaky Smuggling: Axolotls in Danger 50
Fishing for Food: A Tasty Treat 50
Conservation: Saving the Axolotl 50

Conclusion 53

COLORING FUN: LET'S BRING AXOLOTLS TO LIFE! 55

Introduction — Axolotls are Awesome!

Welcome to Axolotls for Kids!

Axolotls sure are interesting animals. They're a bit like a fish and a bit like a lizard. They're kind of like underwater dragons with superpowers! Wait, superpowers? Yes! I mean, do you know of many creatures that live out of the water but can live entirely underwater, look forever young, and... regrow their limbs?! Well, these guys do; they're that cool! Now, because they can live entirely underwater thanks to their gills, and because they also have legs, a lot of people

call them walking fish. But they're actually a type of salamander, which is kind of like a lizard but amphibious. Amphibious means they can live on land as well as in water. These cuties really do get the best of both worlds!

Axolotls come in so many colors and sizes. You can find some as long as a foot, but typically they're about half that size. And while the axolotls you've seen are most likely white and pink, they actually come in a lot of colors like gray, black, or brown with speckles.

They're not just cute and super interesting, they're also pretty important for a lot of reasons. They play a big role in the ecosystems where they live because they control the populations of other creatures. How? Well, they eat insects, small fish, and other invertebrates, helping to keep their numbers under control. And they're also important to science! Scientists around the world are fascinated by their ability to grow their limbs, so they study them to figure out how that happens and then apply that knowledge to our medicine.

In this book, we'll explore their underwater kingdom, we'll talk about their cool and surprising anatomy (their bodies), what they munch on, and their life cycle. Plus, we'll take a closer look at the challenges they face, mainly because of us, and how we can help them by changing a few things. A little effort on our side can go a long way for them!

Ready to embark on this adventure? Let's discover the world of axolotls together!

CHAPTER 1
Axolotls & Their Amazing Amphibian Friends!

AXOLOTLS & THEIR AMAZING AMPHIBIAN FRIENDS!

Axolotls belong to the amphibian family, which, as you may already know, are animals that can live both in water and on land. They start out as aquatic (water) babies with tails and gills, called tadpoles, and grow into adults that can live on land. Most amphibians lose their gills and tails to grow lungs and legs during this change. Axolotls are a bit special in this; you'll soon see why!

Amphibians include a very different group of animals, so we're going to learn about axolotls but also about some of their relatives. By knowing their differences, you'll be able to appreciate how truly amazing they are!

AXOLOTLS: THE MEXICAN MARVEL

Axolotls are scientifically known as Ambystoma mexicanum because they belong in a lake complex near Mexico City. That's their only natural habitat and they wouldn't live anywhere else in the world if humans hadn't brought them there. Pretty cool to think that all the axolotls only ever lived in Mexico City! Now, zoos, animal sanctuaries, and keeping them as pets are the only reasons why there are axolotls in many places outside of Mexico.

Although amphibians can live out of water, axolotls are one of the few species that remain exclusively aquatic throughout their lives. How do they do that? Well, normally amphibians are aquatic and have gills while they're young but lose them when they become adults and change to their terrestrial (land) form. However, axolotls have something called neoteny, which means they keep their gills for their entire life, they're young forever!

There are four main colors of axolotls, although there can be variations when they're mixed together, and they can even have gold speckles! Here are the different types:

- **Albino:** These are the white axolotls with pink gills and reddish eyes. Being albino is much more common in axolotls than in other animals.
- **Leucistic:** Leucistic axolotls are albino axolotls that have black eyes instead of red.
- **Xanthic:** These guys are gray with black eyes.

- **Melanoid:** These axolotls are darker shades of black, olive, or blue with no speckles.

I know those names are a little weird, but they just mean that they can be white or dark colors, with black or reddish eyes. See? Simple!

In the wild, most axolotls are dark-colored with speckled patterns because that helps them blend into the mud and plants of their natural habitat; yes, those colors help them camouflage and hide from other predators. Clever trick! On the other hand, most pet axolotls are albino; which is handy because these pets don't need to hide from predators. They are all different and have their own charm and beauty.

OTHER AMAZING AMPHIBIANS

We've already learned some interesting things about axolotls and there are even more unbelievable ones to come, but before that, do you know other awesome amphibians? Let's get to know some of them!

TIGER SALAMANDER: AXOLOTL'S COUSINS

The tiger salamander is a close relative of the axolotl, and they look pretty much alike while they're young. In fact, when axolotls were first discovered, scientists thought they were tiger salamander babies rather than a different species.

What helped set them apart is that tiger salamanders follow a more traditional amphibian life cycle, starting as aquatic creatures and then changing into terrestrial adults. During this transformation, they have some big changes in their anatomy, including the loss of their gills to develop lungs for breathing air.

Another important difference is that axolotls can only stay out of water for a short time, while tiger salamanders have a mostly terrestrial lifestyle, where they live in burrows and eat insects and small mammals. Despite living on land, they return to the water to lay their eggs to ensure that their young are born underwater. Interesting eh?

FROGS AND TOADS: LEAPING RELATIVES

Frogs and toads are other fascinating members of the amphibian family. Salamanders and axolotls have long bodies and tails, but

frogs and toads have short bodies with no tails. They also have much stronger hind legs than their front ones, which is why they're such amazing jumpers. They can jump as far as fifty times their size to catch food or to escape predators!

Frogs and toads may look similar to each other, but they're certainly not the same. Frogs have smooth and moist skin and live near water bodies. Toads, on the other hand, have dry and warty skin and are adapted to dry environments. But they do have one thing in common: their eggs hatch into tadpoles that eventually lose their tails and gills to grow legs and lungs, moving from an aquatic life to a terrestrial one.

Both frogs and toads both feed on bugs and small animals, which is why they're an important part of their ecosystems. They control insect populations by eating them, but frogs and toads are also food for other larger animals.

As you can see, amphibians may belong to the same family, but they're very different! They all have in common that they start out living in the water with their gills and tails and then change them into lungs and legs to live on land. But there's one amazing creature that defies all this: axolotls! They develop legs and can go out of the water if they need to, but they keep their gills and tails all their lives to be those amazing underwater dragons!

BONUS FACTS!

1. The word "axolotl" is a bit tricky to say, but here's a fun fact: it's pronounced "ACK-suh-LAH-tuhl" and comes from the ancient Aztec language, Nahuatl!

2. Axolotls are the Peter Pan of Salamanders because of their neoteny. This means they keep young features throughout their life, like their gills. And perhaps their little young faces!

3. Axolotls always seem to have a permanent smile due to the structure of their mouths. Too cute!

4. Their name comes from the Aztec god Xolotl, who was associated with lightning and death.

5. Axolotls have existed since the time of the dinosaurs, with some species dating back over 140 million years!

CHAPTER 2

Axolotl Anatomy: Discover Their Wiggly Parts

AXOLOTL ANATOMY: DISCOVER THEIR WIGGLY PARTS

Now that we've met all those fascinating creatures, wouldn't you like to know a little bit more about the parts axolotls are made of? What makes them so special? How can they breathe underwater even when they're adults? We're about to explore the anatomy of your new awesome friends. Let's go!

GILLS: BREATHING UNDERWATER

If there's one body part that axolotls are famous for, it's their gills! I'm sure that when you think of an axolotl, the first thing that comes to your mind are those little fringes on the sides of their head that give them that fun and charming look. They have three gills that look like little feathers on each side of their head. Axolotls use these gills to absorb oxygen from the water and that's how they can breathe underwater.

Axolotls that are dark colored have gills of the same color, but white axolotls (albino) have gills that look pink. How's that possible if being albino means having no color? Well, those gills have very thin skin and are full of tiny blood vessels, that's why they look pink! Axolotls absorb oxygen through these tiny blood vessels, and they can change color if they're feeling a little under the weather. Handy for pet owners!

Although they're almost entirely aquatic thanks to their gills, axolotls also have tiny lungs. Those lungs aren't fully developed, but they allow them to stay out of the water for a few hours. This feature helps them to adapt to their environment very quickly. For example, if their habitat dries up, they can survive until they find another place with water, (so clever!) or they can come out to breathe on land if oxygen levels in the water drop. Wouldn't it be great if you could breathe both in and out of the water? Axolotls are amazing!

LIMBS: TINY FEET, BIG MOVES

Axolotls have four short legs, two on each side of their body. Their front legs have four toes, and their back legs have five, with little claws on all of them. Cute overload! Even though axolotls swim most of the time and their legs are short, those legs are really powerful. They can grab onto rocks, crawl around the bottom, or grab their food to eat.

However, their small legs are not as developed as those of other land amphibians. That's why they can't run as fast as them when they're out of the water. They're a bit clumsy, like a fish out of water!

Axolotls have another amazing ability; they're able to regrow parts of their body and that includes their legs! So, if they get hurt or some predator has an axolotl leg as a snack, they can just grow it back! And we're not talking about growing something that looks like a leg a leg, no. We're talking about them growing everything exactly as it was: bones, muscles, nerves, and skin, even their little claws! Axolotls can do this with any part of their body, not just their legs, and it's a skill that has scientists around the world in awe and pretty puzzled. We'll see more about this a little later!

SKIN: SMOOTH & SLIMY

Axolotls have really smooth skin and they're also a bit slimy. That's because they're covered in mucus that protects them and helps them glide through the water. That mucus protects that thin skin and prevents parasites or infections from attacking them. It's like we're wearing a special suit that doesn't let mosquitoes bite us, how cool!

We've already talked about this, but let's look a little more at the colors of axolotls.

Axolotls have four genetic colors, but they can be mixed and form many combinations.

That's why we find such different axolotls in nature.

Wild axolotls are almost always dark colors like brown or black and are often mottled. Why is that? Because as we said earlier, those colors help them blend in with their environment and escape predators, so those axolotls have a better chance of surviving than others with brighter colors.

Other axolotls can be gray, dark blue, olive, all of them with or without mottling. And they can also be colorless. Albino axolotls are almost all white with red or black eyes (leucistic), but there are some special ones that have shiny skin that makes them look golden! It's also possible to get brighter colors, but that rarely happens in the wild and has more to do with breeding them in captivity or selling them as exotic pets.

Axolotls have very sensitive skin. Anything that happens in their environment or any changes within their body affects their skin. If an axolotl is not in good health, their skin can change color. Likewise, if their habitat has more or less light than usual. Pollution in their habitat or even picking them up with our hands can irritate their skin, so we need to protect both their natural habitats and their pet enclosures. And as cute as they are, we have to give them space and not touch them too much!

BONUS FACTS!

1. Axolotls are sometimes called alien fish due to their weird, otherworldly appearance. We think they look super cute, but some find them a little... freaky looking!
2. Unlike humans, axolotls do not have eyelids, so they can never blink!
3. Axolotls don't have moving tongues like frogs or toads—they swallow their food whole.
4. Axolotls are considered a cultural icon in Mexico, especially in the city of Xochimilco.
5. Their stomachs are only the size of their heads, so they eat frequently but in small amounts.

CHAPTER 3
Axolotl Habitat: Their Magical Water Worlds

AXOLOTL HABITAT: THEIR MAGICAL WATER WORLDS

Unlike other animals, axolotls have very limited habitats. Their natural habitat is quite unique and can only be found in lakes and canals in Mexico. Outside of that, they only live in man-made enclosures around the world, either in zoos, animal sanctuaries, or at home as pets. Understanding their natural habitat is really important in order to create those same conditions and give them everything they need to be happy and healthy.

LAKES AND CANALS: HOME SWEET HOME

Axolotls are native to the Xochimilco and Chalco lakes near Mexico City. Both lakes have been drained for years to prevent flooding in nearby cities. Lake Chalco has already disappeared, and Lake Xochimilco is no longer a large, deep lake, but a series of shallow canals. This natural habitat for axolotls has clear, well-oxygenated (lots of air) waters as well as warm temperatures throughout most of the year.

These canals, while not very deep, have lots of vegetation that gives axolotls places to live, hunt, and hide. These waters are home to plenty of insects, fish, and other amphibians so whenever they're hungry, there are plenty of options on the menu!

Unfortunately, the natural habitat of axolotls is in real danger from water pollution, urban growth, and the introduction of invasive species. These species, mainly fish, are animals that don't belong

in that habitat and are introduced by man. It may seem harmless, but these fish upset the balance of the ecosystem in two different ways: they eat the same food as the axolotls, so there's less for them to eat, or they eat the young axolotls. In both cases, it's sadly become a lot more difficult for the axolotls to survive in their original habitats.

For these and a few more reasons that we'll talk about later, the axolotls are in critical danger of extinction. We need to make some serious conservation efforts if we want to save this incredible species!

AQUARIUMS: WELCOME AXOLOTLS TO THEIR NEW SPLASHY HOME!

The population of axolotls in the wild is getting smaller and smaller, but their charm has made many pet owners all over the world fall in love with them. This way, there are more and more axolotls bred in captivity that help prevent them from disappearing. However, this can have its not-so-good side, since some people who don't do things quite right can hunt them illegally in their natural habitat to sell them as pets. I know, right?

If you decide to have a pet axolotl, the first thing is to make sure that it's been bred in captivity in the best conditions. Once you know that your axolotl hasn't been taken from its habitat, it's time to set up its new home! How exciting! The most important thing is to try to recreate the same conditions it would have in the wild to ensure its health and well-being.

- There needs to be plenty of space for each axolotl.
- They need the same warm temperature that they would have in Mexico.
- It's important to filter the water so that it has enough oxygen, but without creating currents because axolotls love calm waters.
- Make sure they have a lot of hiding spots in their tank to feel safe, you can add decorations such as caves, pipes, and plants!!
- It's important to give them a variety of foods so they have a balanced and nutrient-rich diet. Also, the quantities are very important to prevent them from eating too much.

- Keep their enclosure clean; axolotls produce a lot of waste!

Owning an axolotl can be an amazing experience, they're cute, fun-looking, interesting, and pretty easy to care for. However, you should know that it's a long-term commitment, as axolotls can live up to fifteen years if you take good care of them. With all this in mind, axolotls can have a long, healthy, and happy life indoors!

BONUS FACTS!

1. Axolotls don't like direct sunlight and prefer darker environments since they don't have protective skin to protect them from UV rays.

2. Axolotls are cold-blooded, so they don't need much energy to survive, and they can go weeks without food.

3. Some axolotls, especially albinos, have partially transparent skin, so you can see their organs at work! Super interesting!

4. Axolotls grow larger in captivity than in the wild, with some growing over 18 inches long!

5. Due to their quiet nature and cute appearance, axolotls have become popular pets around the world, especially in recent years.

CHAPTER 4

Yummy Eats for Axolotls: What's on Their Menu?

YUMMY EATS FOR AXOLOTLS: WHAT'S ON THEIR MENU?

Axolotls aren't picky eaters at all, they can eat almost anything! Well, not just anything, they're carnivores so as long as it's some insect, fish, or other small animal, they won't say no if they're hungry! They won't stick up those noses (yes, they do have little nostrils!) at a piece of lettuce though and do enjoy leafy greens as a snack!

INSECTS AND WORMS: YUMMY PROTEIN

In their natural habitat, axolotls have plenty of fish, insects, and other small animals to eat. But their all-time favorites are worms! Axolotls need lots of protein to grow and worms are an easy source of protein to catch. They just open their mouths and suck the worms up like spaghetti!

If you had to guess what one of the axolotls' most developed senses is, would you say smell? Yes! Even though they live underwater, they have a very good sense of smell, and they use it to find food. They move around until they smell their prey, open their mouths, and suck them up. That's really helpful for finding food among plants or mud - worms can't hide from an axolotl's nose!

FISHY DELIGHTS: A SPECIAL TREAT FOR AQUATIC FRIENDS

Occasionally, axolotls will also eat small fish. Although they're not their first choice, they are part of their diet because they provide many nutrients... and they're yummy! It's really impressive to watch axolotls catch fish. They stay still and wait patiently for prey to pass by, or they sneak up on them and catch them.

CANNIBALISM: IT'S GETTING TOO CROWDED IN HERE!

Axolotls usually feed on other species, however, in certain situations, they can eat other axolotls! You see, they need space, food, and oxygen. That's why overcrowded places are really stressful for them.

If there are too many axolotls in a small space or not enough food for everyone, then they're likely to eat each other until they reach some balance. Makes sense! Once there are enough resources for everyone, everything goes back to normal.

PELLET POWER: TASTY BITES

Pet axolotls can also catch their food if we put fish or worms in their enclosure. Axolotls usually eat everything they can get their little claws on, so if we don't know what to put in or how much, our axolotls can eat less or more than they need, making them sick. And we don't want that!

To make sure that pet axolotls, or axolotls in captivity in general, eat a balanced diet with everything they need to grow healthy, we can give them pelleted food. These pellets have a mix of proteins, vitamins, and everything an axolotl needs to grow big, strong, and happy!

Keep in mind that they like eating a bit too much and can also eat more pellets than they really need, so you also have to give them appropriately sized portions. And to make it more fun, you can teach them to eat from your hand! I can already hear you calling out to your parents asking for a pet axolotl!

BONUS FACTS!

1. There's a book that features a story of a man's obsession with axolotls. It's called "The Axolotl's Smile" by Julio Cortázar. Check it out!

2. Do you play Minecraft? Axolotls were introduced in Minecraft in 2021, becoming a fan-favorite for their cute look and helpful nature in water battles.

3. The famous Pokémon Wooper and Mudkip were both based on axolotls, showcasing their amphibious nature. They're adorable!

4. Axolotls have a slow metabolism, which is why they only need to eat a few times a week.

5. Unlike most amphibians, axolotls don't flick their tongues (because they don't have a moving one!) Instead, they use their suction to capture prey.

CHAPTER 5
Axolotl Antics: Discover Their Funny Behaviors

AXOLOTL ANTICS: DISCOVER THEIR FUNNY BEHAVIORS

Among axolotls' behaviors, the most impressive has got to be their ability to regrow body parts! They also have some awesome hunting skills; they're full of surprises! They're clever, sneaky, and curious animals with a unique lifestyle. They're truly remarkable creatures. Let's find out more!

REGENERATION: BEST SKILL EVER

Can you imagine losing a finger, a hand, an ear… and growing a new one in a few days? That's pure science fiction for us, but not for axolotls! These little animals have real superpowers! Most animals, including humans, can heal their wounds, but once we lose a limb it's gone for good. Well, axolotls can regrow entire body parts and not just their legs, but also their tail, and even their heart or brain! How awesome is that?

When an axolotl suffers an accident or a predator attacks them and they lose some part of their body, it takes them just a few days to heal their wounds. They're very fast healers! In a few weeks, between four and six, they're able to create new bones, muscles, nerves, skin… to grow legs with their fingers from scratch. It takes them only three months to create a whole new body part that looks and works exactly as before. And they can do this as many times as they need!

Scientists around the world are studying axolotls and trying to understand all the mechanisms behind this amazing ability. Their goal is to be able to copy this process to heal human injuries. Achieving that would be fantastic news!

SNEAKY PREDATORS: THE ULTIMATE HIDE-AND-GULP HUNTERS!

You already know that axolotls can open their mouths and suck up worms like they're eating pasta. You also know that they wait patiently for small fish to pass by and then…gulp! But how do they know where there are worms, fish, or other food? Well, they have a great sense of smell that helps them find prey among plants and mud, but that's not all!

Axolotls have special cells on their sides that can sense movements and vibrations in the water. They're called the lateral line system. With these cells, they can find fish or other animals even if they can't see or smell them. Axolotls are better predators than they look, aren't they?

By the way, axolotls have very small teeth, so instead of chewing their food, which would take them too long, they swallow it whole!

SOCIAL LIFE: SOLITARY BUT CURIOUS

Axolotls don't need company, they're rather solitary creatures. Other animals live in groups, help each other hunt, or raise their babies together. Axolotls don't; they simply don't have those social behaviors. They may encounter other axolotls while exploring their surroundings, and be curious about them, but they don't live in groups with them. If you have more than one pet axolotl, they can live in the same enclosure, but with enough space for each one to avoid stressing them out.

Although they're solitary creatures, they're curious about other beings. And that includes you! Your pet axolotl can recognize your face and even approach you when you go to feed it or clean its home. So, as long as you don't want to be his tank mate, it's all good!

BONUS FACTS!

1. Axolotls are often used as education ambassadors in zoos and aquariums to promote amphibian conservation efforts.
2. In Aztec mythology, the god Xolotl turned into an axolotl to avoid being sacrificed, making the creature a symbol of transformation and survival.
3. Some axolotl pet owners believe their pets can recognize them based on movement and behavior, making them more interactive than expected.
4. Axolotls are called "water monsters" because they spend their whole lives in the water and look like tiny, smiling sea creatures.
5. Axolotls are more active at night, which is when they like to hunt for food.

CHAPTER 6

Axolotl Life Cycle: From Tiny Egg to Underwater Superstar

AXOLOTL LIFE CYCLE: FROM TINY EGG TO UNDERWATER SUPERSTAR

Since they're just eggs until they grow those cute feathery gills, the life cycle of an axolotl is a fascinating journey! Unlike many other amphibians, as you now know, axolotls don't lose all their juvenile traits, but they keep some of them throughout their lives. This ability is called neoteny; they're neotenic creatures.

EGGS: THE BEGINNING OF LIFE

It all starts with an axolotl mom finding the perfect place to lay her eggs, usually near a plant underwater. A female axolotl lays hundreds of eggs and attaches them to plants or other surfaces so they don't float away. Those eggs are covered in a layer of jelly that protects them from their environment and other animals. The eggs take between two to three weeks to hatch depending on the temperature, the warmer the water, the faster they'll hatch!

LARVAE: GROWING UP UNDERWATER

Once they hatch, the larvae look like mini axolotls without legs! They do have their gills and tails for swimming. They can be larvae for months depending on how much food they can find, and they need to eat a lot to grow! As they grow, they develop legs and start to look like adult axolotls.

Unlike other amphibians, axolotls don't undergo a full transformation to become terrestrial adults. They keep their gills and their finned tail throughout their lives. This neotenic trait allows them to live underwater all the time.

There have been extremely rare cases where they have followed a more traditional change, becoming terrestrial salamanders. However, these have been due to experiments or very extreme changes in their environment.

ADULTHOOD: AXOLOTLS STAY YOUNG FOREVER!

Once they have their limbs fully developed... congratulations, they're adults! But even after they're adults, they still look like they did when they were babies, with their feathery gills and tails. That's what allows them to stay (super cute!) in the water their whole lives and avoid any challenges they might encounter in their life on land.

Axolotls can live for a long time. Pet axolotls live up to fifteen years or more if you take good care of them. That's why many people like to keep them! But in the wild, they usually don't live as long because of predators, pollution, or losing their habitats. As you can see, we're part of the problem but we're about to see that we can also be the solution!

BONUS FACTS!

1. Axolotls need a lot of room in their tanks to swim around happily. They love their space!

2. They can sense movements in the water around them using special lines on their bodies.

3. Axolotls don't need to sleep a lot! They take tiny naps during the day instead of long periods of sleep, like superhero power naps.

4. An axolotl can grow bigger than your hand, but they still look like little babies! They're like forever-giant tadpoles.

5. In the wild, axolotls can blend into their environment and hide from predators by staying super still. It's like they have an invisibility cloak!

CHAPTER 7

Axolotl Superheroes: Battling the Threats They Face

AXOLOTL SUPERHEROES: BATTLING THE THREATS THEY FACE

Despite all their fascinating adaptations and regenerative abilities, axolotls face a lot of threats in the wild. Their natural habitat is quite limited (just a small area near Mexico City), so changes in the environment and many of the things that people do affect them more than other species with larger territories to live in.

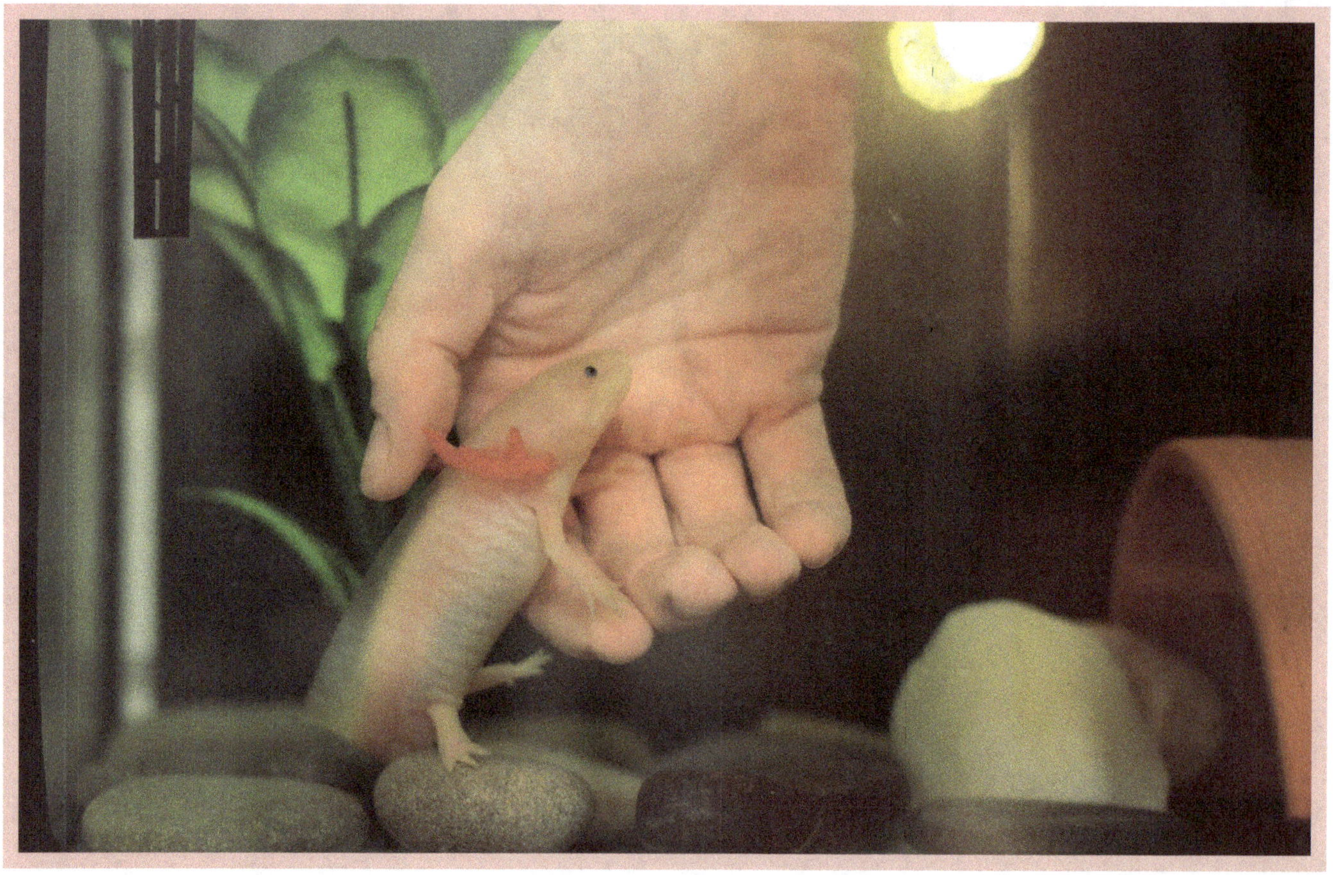

HABITAT DESTRUCTION: AXOLOTLS GOING HOMELESS?

The natural habitat of axolotls is only a lake, so the biggest threat to their survival is losing their home. Once upon a time, there was more than one lake, and they were quite large and deep. As we discussed earlier, the cities around them have grown over time and someone decided to drain those lakes to avoid possible flooding and to have more space to build. Now the axolotls barely have any room left!

POLLUTION: A SILENT KILLER

Human activity such as building cities or farming often pollutes the water. Lakes that used to be clear and clean now have substances in them that harm axolotls. That sensitive skin of theirs can absorb all of these pollutants, which are like poison to them. Also, these changes in the water can damage their gills, making it very difficult for them to breathe.

EXOTIC FISH: UNWELCOME COMPETITION

Sometimes we like exotic animals from other parts of the world and decide to bring them into our environment. They may be nice to look at, but are in fact, dangerous for ecosystems. How's that? Ecosystems live in balance between the amount of food available (plants, small animals…) and the species that live and eat there. If we put a new animal into the mix, it can eat the food of a species that already lived there and make it harder for it to survive. That's what's happening with axolotls!

At some point someone decided to introduce exotic fish into the lake, thinking that they wouldn't do any harm. However, some of these new fish eat the same insects as the axolotls so now there's less food for them. Also, other new fish don't eat their food, but they eat their offspring so that's even worse for their survival.

SNEAKY SMUGGLING: AXOLOTLS IN DANGER

Axolotls have become one of many people's favorite pets. And they cost quite a bit of money! That's why some people can't wait to breed them in captivity and catch them in the wild. But that's just wrong! Catching them illegally endangers their survival in the wild, so it's important to make sure your pet axolotl comes from a place that does things right and does not get them from an axolotl hunter.

FISHING FOR FOOD: A TASTY TREAT

Some people think axolotls are delicious and fish them for food. I know, it's hard to imagine! Keep in mind that different people with different traditions eat different things, so that's not the problem.

The issue here is that there are only a few axolotls left and they don't need the extra threat of people fishing them. Imagine if, besides their natural predators, lots of us humans eat them too! It's likely though, that some people will still eat them because they don't understand the situation, so we should find sustainable solutions like axolotl farms with some serious regulations.

CONSERVATION: SAVING THE AXOLOTL

As you have already learned, in recent years, axolotl populations have dropped. Scientists counted how many axolotls there were in the same amount of water, and they went from over 5,000 to less than 100 in twenty years! And that's not the bad news! The bad news is that shortly after that, they measured again, and they didn't find any

axolotls in the lake! They could only see two axolotls in some nearby canals. That's so worrying, don't you think?

Protecting axolotls is in our hands so what can we do? We must protect their natural habitat and stop destroying it, control water pollution, not introduce invasive species, and teach people to eat them sustainably.

To restore their habitat, we can clean the water from pollutants and create protected spaces where axolotls can grow happily and safely from any threats. And if possible, it'd be fantastic to remove the exotic species that we once put there. This way, with fewer predators and more food available there will be more axolotls in no time!

There are already programs to breed them in captivity and then take them back to the wild, but that's not enough. It's very important to prevent them from being caught in the first place, illegally or overfished, and so we need stronger regulations on that. Sustainable farms and sanctuaries are a good solution to those problems.

And as always, our best tool is education. Awareness campaigns are really important to get people to learn about axolotls, how amazing they are, and how vital it is to protect them! The goal of these campaigns should be to promote responsible human behaviors to reduce our impact on the environment and the natural habitat of axolotls. So, spread the word! Tell everyone how cool they are and how they need to be protected because many people don't even know they are threatened.

BONUS FACTS!

1. There's an anime series with an Axolotl Fruit that gives the user the power to transform into an axolotl. Cool, right?

2. Baby axolotls are sometimes cannibalistic, and breeders often have to separate them to avoid fights.

3. Some axolotls that are genetically modified in labs can glow under special lights, like little water creatures from a science fiction movie.

4. Axolotls absolutely love to eat worms! It's one of their favorite snacks, and they can even eat worms longer than their own heads.

5. Even though axolotls don't have ears like we do, they can still sense vibrations in the water to detect sounds and movements around them!

Conclusion

And here we are at the end of our underwater adventure learning all about amazing axolotls! Axolotls are truly one-of-a-kind creatures, and I bet you've learned a lot of cool things about them.

In this book, you've discovered how interesting they are, from their unique ability to regrow body parts to their way of staying forever young. These little creatures also play a really important role in their environment, helping to keep their ecosystems in balance. By just being themselves, living there, and eating what they like, axolotls help other animals and plants thrive too!

Every axolotl we've talked about shows just how incredible they are. Like the dark-colored ones that blend into their surroundings with their speckled patterns, or the albinos that look like tiny, pink water dragons!

Learning all these things helps us see the world in a whole new way. Axolotls remind us that even the tiniest creatures have big roles in nature. Next time you spot an axolotl in a book, a movie, or a pet store, I'm sure you'll remember how awesome they are. Go you're your friends!

I hope you enjoyed this book and discovered lots of new and exciting things. Keep exploring and learning about the world around you, there's always more to discover!

COLORING FUN: LET'S BRING AXOLOTLS TO LIFE!

www.ingramcontent.com/pod-product-compliance
Lightning Source LLC
Chambersburg PA
CBHW081627100526
44590CB00021B/3629